CHATELAINE
home decor

THE NEW MODERN

THE NEW MODERN

In today's decorating the magic is in the mix

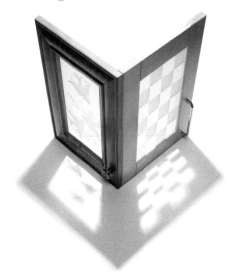

BY JOAN MACKIE

M&S

A SMITH SHERMAN BOOK
produced in conjunction with CHATELAINE®
and published by McCLELLAND & STEWART INC.

CHATELAINE

Canadian Cataloguing in Publication Data

Mackie, Joan
    The New Modern : in today's decorating the magic is in the mix

(Chatelaine home decor)
"A Smith Sherman book produced in conjunction with Chatelaine"
Includes index.

ISBN 0-7710-2013-9

1. Interior Decoration   I. Title.   II. Series.

NK2110.M3 1998   747.2'0499   C98-931776-5

ACKNOWLEDGEMENTS

WRITING *THE NEW MODERN* has been a joyful adventure for me because of all the creative people I've encountered along the way who have made this book possible. First of all, I am very grateful to the homeowners and designers who have graciously consented to let me reproduce their work here.

It has been a pleasure to collaborate once again with Carol Sherman and Andrew Smith of Smith Sherman Books; their creativity and excellence are matched by the pleasure they provide throughout the making of a book.

I am grateful to Rona Maynard, editor of CHATELAINE, for giving me the freedom to create exciting home-decorating features in the magazine each month, and to Group Publisher Lee Simpson for her enthusiastic support of my work. Caren Watkins, CHATELAINE's art director, Ann Shier, associate art director and creative associate Barbara Glaser are always available to help me develop ways of presenting material artistically, and I thank them for that.

My thanks, too, to all the photographers whose pictures appear in this book, especially Ted Yarwood and Evan Dion, who unfailingly and cheerfully put forth their best effort on my behalf.

Thanks to Deborah Aldcorn for her keen eye and attention to detail, Joseph Gisini for his creativity and happy disposition, Erik Tanner for his sage advice, and everyone at McClelland & Stewart.

Finally, I thank my husband, Keith Wagland, for his patience, support, and, in many instances, his physical help in creating beautiful scenarios for the pages of CHATELAINE and this book.

JOAN MACKIE

COVER PHOTO: *see page 28*

PHOTO PAGE 2: *see page 24*

CREDITS: *see page 127*

CONTENTS

continued on next page

BATHROOMS

SPRUCE UP A WINDOW
Use Masonite and wallpaper to breathe life into a ho-hum window.

SHOW-OFF SHOWER CURTAIN
Stitch up a jaunty collared curtain for the shower.

COLOR-PUNCHED TOWEL BARS
A sense of fun freshens up a dated bathroom.

NOTHING TO SNEEZE AT!
Pop a touch of glamour in a bath or bedroom with a silvery tissue box.

HOME OFFICES

FILING CABINET WITH FINESSE
Pressed wallcovering transforms a derelict cabinet into a stunning beauty.

PAPER TRAILER
Put plain wooden boxes to work in a home office.

WELL-DRESSED WINDOW
Pared-down decorating equals easy-to-make window coverings.

SHELVE IT!
Create a basement home office with imagination.

PERSONALITY POP UP
Photographs personalize a tissue box.

HARLEQUIN HOLD-ALL
Keep your notes neatly tucked into a ribbon-laced memo board.

INTRODUCTION

$\mathcal{D}$ECORATING A HOME — whether that home is a condominium, house or apartment — has never been easier, friendlier or more satisfying than it is right now. The New Modern, this perfect-for-the-times decorating style, lets you decorate in ways that please you, using furnishings and accessories that cut through time periods and across trends. Maybe it's something from a previous generation, long lost in the family attic, or a found object from a flea market. Mixed and matched with contemporary furnishings with clean lines, they create the latest look.

The New Modern eliminates the need to live in discomfort for the sake of aesthetics, because it gives you permission to put the pieces together as you want, creating an environment where personal comforts and pleasures are paramount.

This is not to say a jumbled look is the defining criterion. Not at all.

Basic design principles must still be followed for harmony to prevail and satisfying appearances to be achieved. The book you are holding will help you figure out how to get the look and how to decide what works together and what doesn't. *The New Modern* shows you how to create this eclectic elegance with photographs of beautiful rooms whose contents are described and analyzed. Then, for all you hands-on people whose greatest joy in decorating is to make accessories and create interiors, more than 50 projects set you on the path to creating your own New Modern home.

So let sleek meet soft, antiques mingle with contemporary; you will revel in their disparate natures and energizing effect. This look is comfortable, comforting and pleasing; your home will be easier to decorate, easier to live in, easier to love.

Entrances
GREAT BEGINNINGS

A GOOD FIRST impression is no less important in decorating than it is in social or work situations. Designing and furnishing a successful entrance can be an especially challenging exercise if the space is small. With the New Modern decorating style, the door is open to stylishly furnishing all entries, regardless of their size, because you can combine new and old pieces, myriad materials and dramatic details, or pare down to sparse accessories whose intrinsic beauty set the scene for the rest of the house.

An entryway must accommodate owners and guests, who may need to remove boots, hang up hats, lay down parcels or purses, or help a child get out of winter clothing. Because of this, the entry benefits from having a place to hang the coats (pegs will work if no closet is possible), a table for packages and keys (a narrow wall-mounted shelf can substitute if space is tight), somewhere to sit (a chair is best; a space-saving stool will also do) and adequate but artful lighting (bright enough for safety but subdued enough to create a mood). Not all entrance areas can accommodate everything, particularly if the room is very small, but even tiny areas can be fun to decorate.

The creative use of space is important and what's left bare is as significant as the areas that are filled, because minimally appointed rooms, such as the entrances, left, and on page 16, can be as satisfyingly attractive as more lavishly furnished ones, such as on page 17.

The entrance on page 16 shows New Modern traits in its mixture of materials and combination of styles from different

NEW-CENTURY ELEGANCE
Sparse but not Spartan, the entrance of a suburban home greets guests with elegant restraint. Against a backdrop of pale pastel walls and handsomely proportioned moldings, a simple clock, a wooden box and a small bouquet of roses demurely decorate the console table.

periods. Limestone and maple, two materials not often mated, make a sensational flooring treatment. Contemporary curtains balance the antique buffet.

It's another stunning floor that dramatizes and enlarges the perceived size of the entry on page 15. Set on the diagonal, black and white tiles visually push back the walls of the room, a space already enviably large enough for a demi-lune table and a pair of side chairs. The shaded chandelier is a pleasant surprise (a New Modern trait, too), for it's an element more often at home in a dining room than in an entrance. The appearance of an accessory out of its normal context creates a vitality that's prized in today's decorating, and nowhere is it more appropriate than in an entryway, where an energized atmosphere guarantees a warm welcome.

Furnishings that span several periods produce interesting, vibrant environments. When the scale of the pieces is delicate and the walls are painted in a space-creating light color, as in the entrance on page 10, the room feels more spacious than it really is. Larger furniture would balloon out into the small area; dark walls would draw in too closely for comfort. Though formal, the individual items in the room appear relaxed rather than uptight.

And to prove that decorating to please oneself is the most significant aspect of the New Modern, the entrance (right) wins the prize, for here's a room brimming with personality and self-confidence. Spunky stripes, bold marbling, saucy spots on tuck-away stools and made-for-drama wall sconces all issue a bold statement that's clearly joyous. That's what decorating today is all about. ❖

CREATIVE CORRIDOR

A recent renovation removed a parade of archways that
marched from the front to the back of a small house. The
clean lines that now prevail make the space seem larger
and brighter and form a stark contrast to the soft and
inviting scene that beckons from the far end of the corridor.
There, a turn-of-the-century daybed creates a compatible
trip-through-history grouping with a thirties coffee table
and a round skirted table right out of the eighties, all
grounded by a nineties sisal carpet.

WELCOMING WINDOW

As every entrance should, this one hints at how the rest of the
house will look — classic, but friendly and pleasingly personal.
Big enough to hold a party crowd, the welcoming entrance
suggests formality, but an arched window, through which a
large kitchen and family room unfold, knocks the starch out
of any stuffiness. The diagonally patterned floor provides a
theatricality, yet the chandelier softens the seriousness.

COUNTRY MEETS CITY

The accessories may be high style and their arrangement formal, but the way they are combined is relaxed and easy. Elongated candle lamps match the somewhat exaggerated scale of a pair of dried boxwood topiaries. Tin column capitals mounted on the wall turn into decorative shelves. Newly minted chairs and a canvas-covered hall table show how well old and new mix in a small space.

ENTER HERE

An unlikely but harmonious combination of materials and periods in this entrance puts it in the forefront of the New Modern style of decorating. Limestone and maple laid on the diagonal focus attention on the floor, directing the eye either into the house or out to the garden. Soft contemporary curtains swished to one side and held by sumptuous tassels appear casual and jaunty compared with the formality of the antique buffet. None of the elements matches in the traditional sense, yet they come together to create an entrance that brims with warmth.

Entrance
PROJECTS

REFLECTIONS FROM THE PAST
*Put yourself — and your family — in the picture with
a personalized mirror frame.*

1. Paint the frame black, then (if desired) gild it. One method is to use either gold or silver paint. Paint on thinly, then wipe off with a soft rag. Reapply and wipe off several times until the desired look is achieved. A second method is to gild using gold leaf: if using this method, paint the areas to be gilded with size, let dry until tacky, then apply pieces of leaf onto the size, pressing in place using a soft brush. Then wipe away any excess leaf with a dry soft cloth. Paint or gild the frame of the small mirror in the same way.

2. Paint the good side of the Masonite black, applying two or more coats as necessary. Sand until very smooth. Position the Masonite inside the large frame and nail in place on the back side with very small nails.

3. Using carpenters' glue, attach the framed mirror to the Masonite.

4. Arrange the photocopied photographs in a pleasing pattern on the black border of Masonite surrounding the small mirror. (Before photocopying, "frame" the photographs with clip art or computer-generated frames if desired.) Spread a thin layer of white craft glue over the entire back surface of each photocopy and press in place, easing out any air bubbles or excess glue. Wipe away any glue with a damp cloth.

5. Set aside to dry, then apply three coats of matte acrylic varnish over the photocopies and black border, letting dry and lightly sanding between coats.

6. Cut a piece of brown paper ¼ inch (0.5 cm) smaller than the frame. Spread craft glue in a thin line around the perimeter of the paper. Attach it to the back side of the frame. Attach picture wire using eye screws and mount on the wall.

SHOPPING LIST
- *an old or new frame, approximately 36x28 inches (90x70 cm)*
- *two (2 oz/60 mL) bottles black acrylic craft paint*
- *one (2 oz/60 mL) bottle each of gold and silver acrylic craft paint or 6 or 8 sheets gold leaf, plus size (available at art stores)*
- *¼-inch-thick (0.5-cm) Masonite, cut to fit inside the frame*
- *fine sandpaper*
- *small framed mirror*
- *very small nails*
- *carpenters' glue*
- *laser photocopies of family photos*
- *decorative clip art or computer-printed borders or frames (optional)*
- *white craft glue*
- *matte acrylic varnish*
- *brown paper*
- *picture wire and two eye screws*

HIGH LIGHT

With just paper and wire, you can make a ceiling light fixture in under two hours.

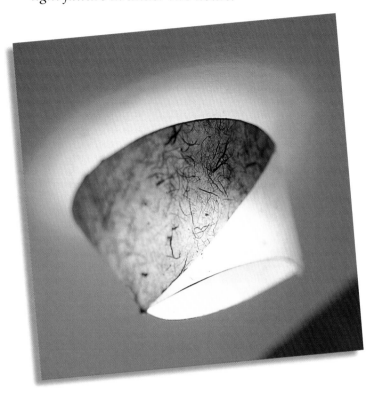

1. Attach one 8-inch (20-cm) rod and one rod cut down to 6½ inches (16.5 cm) to the round wire frame by wrapping the joins with a 6-inch (15-cm) length of fine wire. Cut off the excess wire. Reinforce with a dab of epoxy glue.

2. Form the base of the frame by bending two 8-inch (20-cm) pieces of wire into arcs. Attach to the vertical rods by wrapping with wire and gluing as in the first step. Cut off any lengths of the rods that are sticking above or below the horizontal frames.

3. Before attaching the paper to the frame, be sure the wires of the socket thread properly through the hole in the centre of the top shade frame. Remove while attaching the paper, then replace when you have finished making the shade.

4. Lay the frame on the paper, cut roughly to size. Starting at the top edge of the frame, apply a thin line of tacky glue. Roll the first piece of paper around the wire to attach. Let dry. Cut away excess paper. Cut the second piece of paper roughly to the frame's shape and lay over the first color. Attach the top and bottom edge in the same way as the first.

5. Replace the electrical socket and attach to the ceiling outlet through the ceiling canopy cover.

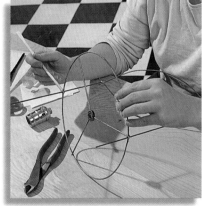

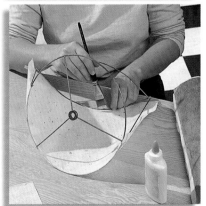

TASSEL ACCENTS

Make them yourself to match your decor.

To make a basic tassel

1. Decide how long you want the tassel to be. Cut a piece of heavy cardboard that measurement deep and about 6 inches (15 cm) wide. Wrap yarn, string or twine around the cardboard. For a slim tassel, wrap it about 20 times; for a medium tassel, wrap it about 30 times and for a thick tassel, wrap it 40 or 50 times.

2. Cut a piece of yarn 12 inches (30 cm) long; fold it in half. Knot it 3 inches (8 cm) from the fold, to create a 3-inch (8-cm) loop. Slip one of the ends under the wrapped yarn at the top edge and tie firmly with a double knot. Position the loop on the outside and tuck the two ends under the wrapped yarn.

3. Carefully pull the cardboard out. Cut a piece of yarn 1 yard (1 m) long. Hold the yarn against the top of the tassel so that one end reaches the bottom edge of the tassel. Form a small loop from the yarn at the top of the tassel and hold firmly in place while using the remaining yarn to wind tightly around the tassel, about 1 inch (2.5 cm) from the top. Keep the loop above the winding yarn.

4. When almost all the yarn has been used, insert the end of it through the loop formed by the starting end of the yarn. Firmly but carefully pull on the end that rests at the bottom edge of the tassel until the loop slips under the wrapped yarn.

5. Using sharp scissors, cut through the bottom tassel loops. Fluff out and neaten the ends so they are even.

TO MAKE THE TINY GOLD TASSEL: Wind cord around a 2-inch-deep (5-cm) piece of cardboard to create a medium-thick tassel, following the directions on the left. After cutting the bottom loops, unravel the cord and comb through it. Attach fabric rosebuds with hot glue. Glue on cord to hang the tassel.

TO MAKE THE BALL-FRINGE-TRIMMED TASSEL: Wind yarn around a 6-inch-deep (15-cm) piece of cardboard to create a thick tassel, following the directions on the left. After cutting the bottom loops, flip the tassel upside down so the yarn falls evenly over the top; wind a 12-inch (30-cm) piece of yarn firmly around the newly created top, forming a head about 1-inch (2.5-cm) deep. Hot glue contrasting fringe around the "neck," then glue fabric balls where shown. Glue on a velvet ribbon to hang the tassel.

FOR A FEATHER-EMBELLISHED TASSEL: Buy a 1-yard (1-m) strip of feather trim at a dressmaker's supply store. Wind around a tassel form, attaching it with hot glue as you wind, until the desired thickness is reached. Attach fabric flowers along the seam line using hot glue. Tie two bows from wired ribbon and glue in place. Glue on a fabric loop to the top of the tassel.

HIGH-TECH MIRROR

Create a contemporary mirror with an industrial spin.

1. Be sure to work in a well-ventilated area. Remove the mirror from its frame, saving the hanging wire and the nails that hold the mirror in place.

2. Paint one coat of acrylic craft paint over the frame. Let dry.

3. Following the directions on the can of spray paint, spray two or three coats of paint over the frame, allowing it to dry thoroughly between coats.

4. Using a hot-glue gun, attach acorn nuts as desired around the frame.

5. Replace the mirror in the frame and hang.

SHOPPING LIST
- *wood-framed mirror, approximately 24x20 inches (61x51 cm)*
- *one (2 oz/60 mL) bottle black acrylic craft paint*
- *one spray can black metallic automobile paint*
- *stainless steel acorn nuts (approximately 18)*
- *hot-glue gun and glue sticks*

TETHERED-LEATHER MIRROR

For a pared-down look, leather is the best.

1. Remove the mirror from its frame, saving the hanging wire and the nails that hold the mirror in place.

2. Place the frame on the underside of the leather and trace around it. Allowing for enough leather to turn under to the back of the frame, cut out the leather required. Clip into the inner corners of the excess leather to make for a neat turn-under where the mirror will be set.

3. Using several colors of crayons, make random markings on the right side of the leather. Immediately smudge the crayon markings with a soft rag.

4. Lay the leather wrong-side up on a flat surface. Top with the frame, then bring the leather to the back of the frame and glue in place with a thin line of hot glue.

5. Reposition the mirror and hold firmly in place with nails and a little hot glue, if necessary.

6. On the right side of the frame, hammer eight nails as shown in the picture. Wind thin cord around a nail several times, stretch it taut to the next nail and wind around it several times again. Keep the ends of the cord in place with a little dab of white craft glue.

7. When the glue holding the cord in place is dry, snip off the ends of the nails and any loose ends of cord.

8. Replace the hanging wire and mount on the wall.

SHOPPING LIST

- *framed mirror, approximately 24x20 inches (61x51 cm) preferably with a flat wood frame with no ridges or curves*
- *piece of cream-colored leather, slightly larger than the frame*
- *crayons*
- *soft rag*
- *hot-glue gun and glue sticks*
- *eight short thin nails and a hammer*
- *thin black cord, approximately 3½ yards (3.2 m)*
- *white craft glue*
- *wire cutter*

Living Rooms
COMFORT ZONES

SINCE LIVING ROOMS are meant to be lived in and are the rooms used when entertaining friends, they deserve to be decorated in the most comfortable and visually pleasing manner. With the New Modern style, it's never been easier.

The living room should contain everything necessary to make its occupants happy: a harmonious color scheme, comfy seating and appropriate lighting for both overall ambiance and individual needs, such as reading and TV viewing. Add to this, pleasing art work, tables positioned to serve adjacent chairs or to embellish a wall and topped with cherished mementoes and decorative accessories, and flooring that provides both visual stimulation and physical comfort underfoot.

The New Modern style of decorating endorses a relaxed approach. The background colors of walls, preferably plucked from a color scheme that appears in window coverings, upholstery or cushions, might be based on energizing yellow or red tones or they may be shades of relaxing greens or blues. If the room is small, light paint colors — or wallcoverings that have small overall patterns — will visually expand the space. Light-colored carpeting or bleached-wood floors, lightweight window coverings and small-scale furniture — a combination of both antique and contemporary pieces — will also make the room appear larger than it is. Avoiding a sense of busy-ness (as often happens when too many disparate items are crowded together) will also help a smallish room seem larger.

The living room that is large and has a high ceiling can be

HIGH STYLE OFF THE PEG
In a room that shows egalitarian elegance, low tech meets high style and mingles with characteristic New Modern friendliness. Silk fabric pegged along sisal twine creates a classy backdrop and a cozy cure for an otherwise problematic room. Wooden dowels mounted on imperfect and cracked walls hold the twine rigid. Clothespins come off the laundry line to peg the lightweight fabric in place. Hardware-store chain suspends expensive architectural prints in yet another high-brow/low-cost mating. Cutting across many time periods and through assorted decorating styles, traditional tapestries and antique furniture live happily with rough sisal carpeting and a cool contemporary lamp.

TIMELESS COMFORT

Pared-down doesn't necessarily mean bare-boned, but the editing process that informs the New Modern eliminates embellishments that in recent decades would have adorned walls and surfaces, thereby freeing the eye to appreciate the beauty of individual elements. Periods and styles combine in a multifunctional space: the newly minted chandelier romances Regency chairs; a wooden writing case and 19th-century lustre-ware plates top a modern repro chest. Textures meet and mingle: silk, taffeta, cane and iron; a wool carpet softens a sisal rug. Comfort reigns in a please-the-owner room.

warmed up by furnishing with rich intense colors. Large-scale furniture, especially in darker shades, and roughly textured fabrics and carpeting will seem to fill up a large space and bring it down to size. With today's decorating, however, there is nothing wrong with leaving space to breathe in a room, even a large one. A sense of space is often the path to comfort, one of the prime qualifiers in today's look.

Living room furnishings and accessories borrowed from several eras eliminate any chance that the room will appear static or frozen in time, and will make it a more interesting space, as the room on pages 26 and 27 shows. Variously colored woods, plenty of patterns and textures and myriad materials and surfaces guarantee an energy that is appealing and comforting, because these all suggest a timelessness and endurance that cosset us all. Even one antique item in an otherwise contemporary room or a single contemporary item in a traditional room will inject a zing into a space, as do the armoire in the living room

FEEL-GOOD DECOR

An engaging mix of furnishings in a low-budget setting comes across with panache and proves that, if you decorate with things you like from several eras and arrange them artfully, the result will be a pleasant environment in which you'll be happy to live. Canvas cover-ups on the loveseat provide the inspiration for stunning-but-simple draperies. A slipcover fashioned from forties drapery fabric hides a metal folding chair from the same period. Glass-top, metal-base tables simply dressed with a few favorite accessories — both new and old — and the organic look of a sisal carpet and wicker boxes make this a comfort-rich room.

CONTEMPORARY MEETS CAST-OFF

A have-it-all bed-sit shows what makes decorating today so appealing. The eclectic mix of good designs bears analyzing. Up-to-the-minute smartly styled, mass-produced tables, chests, desk and lighting mingle artfully with classic leather-and-chrome chairs studded with timeless leopard-print cushions; cast-off bedspreads convert to window coverings and a cozy pumpkin color on the walls holds it all warmly together. There is a surfeit of textures: kilim cushion covers, a sleek laminate bureau, glass-top table, wicker baskets and canvas fabric throughout.

DOLLAR-DRIVEN DECORATING

Invoking a three-pronged decorating motto — reuse, recover and reinvent — produces a dramatic New Modern room on a budget. This decorating scheme features furniture with a past. Fresh upholstery and slipcovers and a little buffing bring everything up to snuff. Challenging those who say a coffee table should be a single item, two mismatched tables and a wicker footstool gather in front of the sofa. The console table pressed to the wall combines a hollow-core door and four wooden wastebaskets; the window coverings feature fibreglass panels suspended from hardware-store chains. In a final flourish, the inspired "carpet" relies on a budget-minded rubber stamp and paint for its existence.

PERSONAL EXPRESSION
A leather sofa and a pine armoire, wool-upholstered chairs, metal cabinet and a glass-top table — strong elements in themselves and decidedly dissimilar — are held together in a room by crown moldings at the ceiling and a sculpted wool carpet underfoot. True to good design principles, the items are balanced in weight and scale; a mixture of light and dark colors create visual interest. Family-favorite accessories express the owners' casual lifestyle and call for comfort foremost.

above and the balance lamp in the living room on page 24.

Funky elements perform the same task of keeping seriousness at bay and suggesting the room has its own personality. At first glance, the living room on page 33 seems static and stiff, ever-so elegant and formidably formal until you realize that its expensive silk curtains swing from hardware-store bathtub chains mounted on a track hidden by a polished steel valance!

The very contemporary room on pages 34 and 35 brims with New Modern characteristics such as mixed materials, multiple textures and relaxed mood. It, too, has funky touches: the harlequin-pattern chest and the hand-crafted African stool, which add a personality punch to the room.

Mining the attic or burrowing in the basement for hidden treasures is guaranteed to turn up something that will up the interest quotient in a living room. For proof, see the vintage typewriter and old dressmaker's "Judy" in the fabulous fifties-inspired room on pages 38 and 39. They prove that no object should immediately be discarded as a potential decorating element and that every piece should be considered on its own merits, which can include simply the fact that you like it or have fond memories of it. ❖

SLEEK CHIC

Mixing materials in a monochromatic setting injects energy into an otherwise all-pervasive calm. Count them: polished steel in the drapery valance, a brushed-aluminum picture frame, a marble fireplace and a combination of pear wood, marble and stainless-steel tables, a wool carpet and hardwood flooring. This respect for materials and pure lines is an important expression of the New Modern design sense. In today's decorating, too, funky is fashionable. How else can one rationalize bath-stopper chains used as high-end decorating elements when paired with expensive silk draperies?

HIGH-CONTRAST CONTEMPORARY
Cushioned comfort softens sleek lines and proves that
a smartly designed space creates room for air without
looking half-decorated. The cozy-up factor of the
streamlined sofa, wicker chairs and sisal rug cannot be
overlooked when exploring the elements that put this
room in the vanguard of the New Modern style. The
curves of the coffee table balance the angles on the
harlequin chest and its stand. There's an energy
generated by the mix of the contemporary lights and
armoire with the tribal influences of the carved stool
and block of framed prints. Never cluttered, the room
spells out warmed-up simplicity.

CUTTING-EDGE COZY

Layering pared-down furniture with selective design-rich accessories means that neither comfort nor style is lost. The mix is in the materials and colors: sleek wood tables, wicker, natural fibres in the fabrics and rug and light colors played against dark walls. The repeated appearance of metal objects offers an edge that deters boredom.

RETRO CHIC

An updated bobby-soxer look, injected with contemporary furnishings, preserves the best from the past and mixes it with "now" accents. Slipper chairs slipcovered in lime green canvas anchor the room; the same fabric accents the stylish window coverings that are threaded onto tension wire. Mining the attic for artifacts turns up a vintage typewriter and sculptural dressmaker's "Judy," which are viewed as art in New Modern settings.

Living Room
PROJECTS

TURN ON A TABLE

Use four wallpaper patterns to turn a plain pedestal table into a showstopping piece.

1. Lightly sand the table to remove or roughen the varnished surface.

2. Place the table upside down on the papers. Trace the circumference of the top and mark where to cut out the desired shapes from each of the papers.

3. Cut out the paper shapes.

4. Glue on the pieces for the first layer; press firmly in place. Let dry, then glue the remaining layers in the same way. If you wish, paint on accents.

5. Apply three coats of urethane, allowing each to dry thoroughly and lightly sanding between coats, if necessary.

SHOPPING LIST
- *plain table*
- *fine sandpaper*
- *large piece of craft paper or newspaper*
- *four or more different wallpaper patterns*
- *sharp scissors or utility knife*
- *white craft glue*
- *semigloss urethane*
- *2-inch (5-cm) paintbrush*
- *paint for detail accents (optional)*

FOOL-THE-EYE FLOOR

Create a faux terrazzo floor with paint and a marker pen.

1. Spray the Aspenite floor with several coats of grey paint, allowing to dry between coats.

2. Using a metal straight edge and pencil, score off large square blocks over the entire floor. The size of the squares depends on the size of the room; 2- to 3-foot (0.6- to 1-m) squares are a good size.

3. Use a marker pen and a straight edge to define the blocks, drawing over the pencil lines.

4. Apply three coats of varnish, allowing to dry between coats.

STYLISHLY SQUARE

Upscale and elegant, this cushion is quick to knit.

SHOPPING LIST

- *Patons Classic Wool Merino Blend: two (100-g) balls ivory (#202); one (100-g) ball grey (#225)*
- *pair 4.5 mm (old Canadian size 7, U.S. 7) knitting needles, or the size needed for tension of 20 stitches and 26 rows measuring 4 inches (10 cm)*
- *darning needle*
- *14-inch (35-cm) cushion form*

1. Using ivory wool, cast on 70 stitches.

2. Work in stocking stitch (knit on right side, purl on wrong side) until the piece measures 5 inches (12.5 cm).

3. The next row will set the color pattern: knit 25 stitches with the ivory wool, join the grey wool and use it to knit the next 20 stitches. Join the second ball of ivory wool and knit the remaining 25 stitches. When changing colors, twist the yarns around each other at the back so holes don't form.

4. Continue in stocking-stitch pattern with the grey block in the centre for a total of 26 rows or until the grey area measures 4 inches (10 cm).

5. Work in stocking stitch with the ivory wool across all stitches for 5 inches (12.5 cm). Cast off.

6. Knit the back of the cushion the same as the front. Sew in loose ends.

7. Block the pieces into 14-inch (35-cm) squares by laying them wrong-side up on an ironing board. Cover with a damp cloth; press lightly using a medium-hot iron. Using the ivory wool, sew three side seams together on the wrong side. Turn right-side out. Stuff with the cushion form. Sew the remaining edge closed.

SCREEN ASSEMBLY

All you need are four ingredients and an hour's work for this project.

1. Select the size and number of stretchers you require based on the height and width of screen desired. This one has four panels, 31x20 inches (70.5x50 cm)

2. Cut paper to fit so you can wrap it around to the back of the stretchers.

3. Use a staple gun to attach the paper to the stretchers in several places. Make neat turns at the corners.

4. Screw two small hinges to each panel to attach them together.

PAINT UP A PLAIN GRASS CARPET

Create a custom look out of a cheapo carpet.

This treatment is not recommended for a carpet in a high-traffic area.

1. Sew carpet squares together using linen thread — if they are not already joined as one piece. Place the carpet on several thicknesses of newspaper.

2. Using latex paint and a roller or brush, paint the desired pattern onto the carpet. Let dry, then apply latex varnish to the painted area.

Chic Window Covering

Simple treatment suits contemporary settings.

Shopping List

- plain canvas or other heavyweight cotton fabric in two colors
- matching thread
- iron-on interfacing (optional)
- metal grommets, at least ½ inch (1 cm) in diameter, but preferably 1 inch (2.5 cm)
- Frekvens hardware system for window coverings, available at IKEA, or heavy wire, sometimes called aircraft cable, two turn buckles and two eye screws, all available at hardware stores

This window treatment works where a window is flanked by walls immediately to either side or where the covering can be inset into the window frame.

1. Measure the size of the window to be covered and calculate the amount of fabric required. You will need twice the width of the window opening in order to provide fullness, and enough extra fabric for hems top and bottom. Calculate the requirements for fabric for the lower border, which should be approximately 15 inches (38 cm) deep. Cut the fabric for the top and lower portions of each panel. Sew together in order to treat the fabric as one piece. Press the seams open.

2. Sew the panels together, if required, to give the correct fullness; press the seams open. Sew double hems 1 inch (2.5 cm) wide along the side edges. Press under ½ inch (1 cm) at the top, then fold again to create a hem 5 inches (12.5 cm) deep. Sew in place. (If desired, a 5-inch (12.5-cm) strip of interfacing may be ironed in place before stitching.) Press under ½ inch (1 cm) along the lower edges, then again to create a 3-inch (8-cm) hem. Sew in place.

3. Punch grommets in the top hem, approximately 4 inches (10 cm) from the top and approximately 8 inches (20 cm) apart.

4. Mount the hardware, thread the wire through the grommets and hang the coverings in place.

GLASS ACT

Turn a plain table into a one-of-a-kind piece. Or try this easy method on other glass surfaces, such as shelves or door windows.

SHOPPING LIST

- *table with a glass top*
- *large sheet of white paper*
- *masking tape*
- *artist's paintbrush*
- *small jar each of gold and bronze Sheffield Lacquer Paint or acrylic craft paint*
- *low-tack translucent masking film (available at art stores)*
- *small art knife*
- *three spray cans of enamel touch-up paint for cars*
- *paint thinner*

1. Work in a well-ventilated room and cover the work surface with newspaper. Trace around the glass onto a large sheet of white paper, then draw a pattern on the paper. Stick the masking tape around the edge of the glass; lay the drawing under the glass. Clean the glass thoroughly.

2. If following the design pictured, paint gold and bronze lines and dots on the glass. Let dry for several hours or overnight.

3. Apply the masking film over the entire surface of the painted side of the glass. Use an art knife to incise the masking film along the lines of the pattern. Lift one section of the film and spray the glass with green touch-up paint, following directions on the can. Let dry. Repeat with the second section of the film using blue paint. Let dry. Lift the third section, spray with turquoise paint. When dry, remove the centre section of the film. Remove any sticky residue with paint thinner.

4. Turn the glass, painted-side down, and set on the wicker table. If needed, small clear bumper pads can be glued on to keep the painted surface from rubbing against the wicker.

CLASSY TRASH

Make a table with wastebaskets and a door.

SHOPPING LIST

- *four wood wastebaskets*
- *18-inch-wide (45-cm) hardboard hollow-core door*
- *two nuts*
- *two washers*

Buy a standard 18-inch-wide (45-cm) hardboard hollow-core door and four wooden wastebaskets with tapered sides. Stack the baskets, attach the bottoms together with nuts and washers, and top with the door for a stunning, minimalist console table. Accessorize as you please!

LOFT-LOOK CHIC

Hang fibreglass panels for the latest look.

1. Determine the number of panels required to cover the window opening. Panels are usually 4 feet (1.2 m) wide and 8 feet (2.4 m) high. The panels should overlap each other by approximately 2 inches (5 cm).

2. Prop the panels against the wall in front of the window where you want them to hang and mark on the top corners where you'll drill holes for the chains that will suspend them. Use a ½-inch (1-cm) drill bit or appropriate bit to create an opening for the chain to pass through. Drill two openings on each panel, in the identical place on each, in both upper corners.

3. Determine where to attach the hooks on the wall above the window opening. You'll want to see at least 4 inches (10 cm) of chain between the hooks and the panels; more is all right, too. The panels should barely touch the floor. Screw the hooks into the wall.

4. Cut the chain pieces ½ inch (1 cm) longer than double the length required to hang them at the desired height. Position two adjacent panels overlapping each other so the corner holes match and pass a piece of chain through the holes. Overlap the ends of the chain by ½ inch (1 cm) and attach together with a key ring. When all the panels are joined, hang by chain loops over the hooks.

ART FORM

No money to frame pictures?
Here's an inexpensive solution.

1. Prop the door against the wall. Using double-sided tape, attach prints or posters to the door.

2. Use acrylic craft paint to define a "frame" around the pictures, if you want. Or leave plain if you plan to use the mounting board for a changing art exhibition.

FAUX FLOOR TREATMENT

Customize laminate flooring with a make-believe carpet.

This treatment will only work on a laminate floor and is not recommended for use in high-traffic areas. For hardwood, it is necessary to remove all varnish or wax to expose the bare wood surface before stamping.

1. Use painters' tape to mark on the floor where the carpet will be stamped. Lay tape along the outer edge first. To create a 3-inch (8-cm) border, press a second line of tape on the floor, 3 inches (8 cm) in from the first tape. Calculate the distance required to stamp the main pattern, then press another line of tape that distance from the second tape in toward the centre of the "carpet." To create an inner border 1½ inches (4 cm) wide, lay a fourth piece of tape 1½ inches (4 cm) from the third piece.

2. Sand within the lines to create a slightly roughened surface to help the paint adhere.

3. Pour paint into the tray, dip the roller into it until it is evenly coated, then pass the roller over the stamp several times to spread a thin layer of paint evenly over the design.

4. Press the stamp on the floor, lift it off carefully, roll on more paint, stamp adjacent to the first mark and continue until the pattern completely fills the border. Let dry.

5. Use the roller to paint between the tapes to create the two solid borders. Let the paint dry. It may be necessary to apply a second coat of paint to the borders. It is not possible to apply a second coat to the stamped areas.

6. When the paint is dry, carefully peel away the tape. Touch up any paint that may have come away with the tape.

7. Use a fresh roller to apply three coats of varnish to the stamped area, allowing to dry between coats.

HOLD YOUR FIRE

Block out the black hole of an unused fireplace with a fancy firescreen.

1. Cut the Masonite with a jigsaw exactly to fit inside the fireplace opening. (Use newspaper to create a pattern if the shape is irregular, then trace it onto the Masonite.)

2. Select an image from a book of architectural drawings or architectural elements which is roughly the same shape and proportion as the fireplace opening. Take it to a reproduction shop and have it blown up to the exact size you require.

3. Lay the Masonite on top of the image and using a pencil, lightly draw around the shape. Cut out the blow-up, allowing an extra inch all around to tuck to the underside. Clip around the corners and curves so the paper will turn under smoothly.

4. Lay the Masonite smooth-side up on a flat work surface. Spread with a thin layer of glue. Carefully position the photocopied image in place. Smooth out any bubbles. Turn the edges to the underside and glue firmly in place.

5. Set against the opening of a fireplace. If necessary, glue a block of wood to the back side to make it stand up properly.

FRAMED!

Two new and novel ways to add interest to framed pictures.

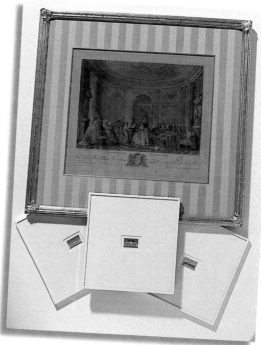

FOR THE STRIPED MATS: Dismantle the frame and remove the mat. Using a very light pencil mark and the ruler, make a faint line where the stripes are to be painted. Paint alternate strips with watercolors. When dry, reassemble the frame.

FOR THE POSTAGE STAMPS: Mount a colorful stamp on a piece of heavy white paper using craft glue and take it to a framing shop. Have it framed with a wide mat, cut to reveal only the stamp plus a small border of the paper backing. Hang a series of three or a group of four framed stamps for a big impact.

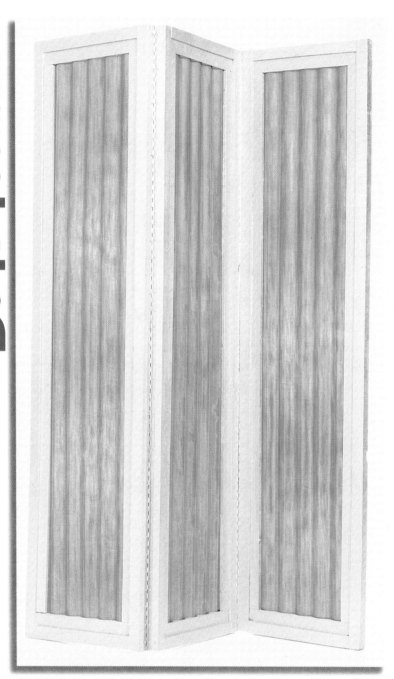

FIBREGLASS SCREEN GEM

For anyone young-at-heart, this funky fibreglass screen adds drama anywhere in the house.

SHOPPING LIST

- *three fibreglass panels, 96x26 inches (2.4x0.65 m)*
- *six 2x2 boards, each 8 feet*
- *corrugated wood strip, approximately 17 feet*
- *six strips half-round wood molding to fit panel corrugations*
- *two piano hinges*
- *24 3-inch (7.5-cm) wood screws*
- *48 2-inch (5-cm) wood screws*
- *42 ¾-inch (2-cm) wood screws*
- *masking tape*
- *three spray cans metallic automobile paint*

---

1. Cut six 72-inch (1.8 m) pieces from 2x2s. From the leftovers, cut six 15-inch (37.5-cm) pieces. Attach with 3-inch (8-cm) screws to form three rectangular frames.

2. Place the frame on top of the fibreglass panel, centring the corrugations. Trace the frame's interior dimensions onto the fibreglass and cut with old scissors. Repeat for the remaining panels.

3. Cut six 69-inch (1.7-m) pieces from the half-round wood molding. Inset approximately ¼ inch (0.5 cm) on the frame, and attach with 2-inch (5-cm) screws, leaving equal space at both ends of each frame.

4. Set each frame face-down, placing the fibreglass inside, and hold with masking tape. Flip the panel over. Measure and cut corrugated wood strips to fill gaps at

the top and bottom of the frame. Ensure corrugations of the wood and fibreglass correspond.

5. Remove the tape and fibreglass. Using 2-inch (5-cm) screws, attach corrugated wood strips.

6. Paint the frames with three coats and let dry between coats. Then install the panels: first, cut six pieces of corrugated wood trim to fit at the top and bottom of each frame at the back. Place each frame face-down: set the fibreglass into the frames. Install the corrugated wood trim using ¾-inch (2-cm) screws at the top and bottom of the screen.

7. Join the panels with piano hinges so that one opens to the front and the other opens to the back, to give the screen stability.

Découpage Screen

Find an art book on sale and create this decorative screen.

I. Select pictures from magazines or old books, enlarge some on a color photocopier, cut out and use to create an arrangement.

2. Cover both sides of the boards with latex primer, then apply several coats of paint. Sand between each coat.

3. To make gold leaf decorations, paint areas where the leaf is to be applied with size (an artists' medium), let dry until tacky, then apply gold leaf. (Or simply paint with gold acrylic paint.)

4. Glue the pictures on the panels according to your plan.

5. When dry, apply three coats of urethane, letting dry and then sanding between each coat.

6. Glue bendable fake wood trim on the top edges, and baseboard trim at the bottom. Bevel the baseboard trim at the side edges.

7. Join the panels with hinges so that one opens to the front and the next opens to the back, to give the screen stability. Screw gold-painted wooden knobs to the tops of the panels with dowels as shown.

Shopping List

- *pictures and color photocopies*
- *five panels of 1-inch-thick (2.5-cm) medium-density fibreboard (have the lumber-yard cut boards 14 inches (35 cm) wide and three heights: one at 6 feet (1.8 m), two at 5 feet 8 inches (1.7 m) and two at 5 feet 4 inches (1.6 m). Use a jigsaw to make the curved top.)*
- *1 quart (1 litre) can each latex primer, paint and urethane*
- *gold leaf and size, available at art supply stores, or gold paint*
- *white craft glue*
- *sandpaper*
- *¾-inch (2-cm) bendable fake wood trim and baseboard trim*
- *12 brass hinges*
- *four wooden knobs and dowels*

Dining Rooms
PLACE SETTINGS

ENTERTAINING IS MORE relaxed than in the past; stiff formality has been abandoned, so the dining room is the perfect place for the New Modern style.

Now you can indulge in mixing pedigreed possessions with contemporary kitsch. Here you can find aesthetic interest in mismatched objects rather than in perfect co-ordination. Here an engaging mixture of furniture and accessories will put everyone at ease. You can be as dramatic or as laid-back as you want, for today the buzz phrase is no more dictatorial decorating!

Comfort and cosseting are key to a satisfying dining room. The deep aubergine walls in the room on page 61 create a warm intimacy for diners gathered around the ultra-modern glass-top table. The chairs — slim-lined and leather-covered or ornate and historically inspired — have little in common except for scale. On the wall and at the window, a painting and draperies with traditional overtones continue to mix the message. Is this a contemporary room or a traditional room? The answer is that it's sort of neither and it's somewhat both, but most of all, it doesn't matter which, because these terms no longer are the defining labels.

RELAXED DINING
Proving that eclectic decorating is successful when the incongruous items are selectively chosen with care, discarded office chairs and an oak table play against a spidery metal chandelier and swishy New Age fabric curtain threaded onto a high-tech tension-wire system. The sense of relaxation that results from such a grouping reflects the owner's style of casual hospitality, yet the sense of design evident in planning the space is never compromised.

MODERN MASTERY

Underpinned by a felt carpet that provides a
hit of color, a twin pedestal table shimmers,
its unique metallic-leaf treatment boldly
exhibiting the join marks of the leaves. Showing
mastery in strong simple design, unadorned
upholstered chairs rim the table, their ebonied
legs acting as a bridge between the cream
fabric and the splashes of hues beneath. Only
one other piece of furniture decorates this
edited-down room: the matching buffet.

EURO-CHIC COMFORT

A masterful mix of unrelated elements turns a
boxy room into a dynamic dining area. Blessed
with a corner doorway, the room conveys a
sense of intrigue and intimacy, tucked away
behind a calico curtain that swags the opening.
A faux marble top elevates the status of a metal
twig-base table. Country-look plaid fabric on
the chairs lessens the seriousness of the room's
dominating feature: the classic fireplace. In true
New Modern style, contemporary glassware and
candlesticks co-exist with family portraits and
brassware from an earlier century.

This is a room — decorated to please — crossing time lines and mixing materials in the New Modern way.

The dining room (opposite) does likewise, although at first glance it appears to be a modern room. Curved frosted-glass windows, marble terrazzo flooring, wire-strung halogen lighting and pared-down accessories on the table add up to a clutch of contemporary characteristics. But look again: the table is a heavy oak, claw-foot Edwardian masterpiece from the early 1900s. The chairs are timeless: bentwood-and-cane classics, made in the sixties to a late 19th-century design. The warmth of these pieces counteracts the coolness of the floor and window wall. The continued use of curved shapes (the wall, table, chair seats and arms) sweep up dinner guests in a metaphorical welcoming hug. The openness of the space further exemplifies a New Modern trait.

Comfort and casualness inform the dining room on page 52 — effects achieved through mixed materials and myriad styles. An oak table straight out of a forties dining room anchors the room; comfy, curved-arm chairs guarantee a pleasant, relaxed dining experience. Nobody gets concerned that the chairs had a previous life in an office setting. Overhead, an end-of-the-century (the 20th century, that is!) lamp casts a warm glow on the tabletop and bathes the room with soft light. New Age fabric in muted colors slides across tension wire to close off the kitchen. This dining room, as the others in this chapter, is please-yourself decorating at its best. ❖

CURVES WITH VERVE
Cooled by a curved wall of pebbled-glass windows and a marble terrazzo-tile floor, a thoroughly modern room gets a warm-up from an Edwardian oak pedestal dining table surrounded by classic bentwood-and-cane chairs. The clean-lined simplicity of the room and the contemporary table-top accessories work because of a successful mix of materials, styles and periods — and the fact that the space left bare is as important as the furnishings.

MIRRORED IMAGE

Jet-black walls create instant theatre in a tiny dining room. A mirrored wall doubles the drama; the swagged and glamorous gold silk curtain reflects light from the chandelier, whose 12-branch shaded lights cast a sparkle on the pattern in the chair upholstery. No one style dominates the room; it's the eclectic mix of dramatic elements that makes it work.

MIXED STYLES

A modern marble table bearing little ornamentation mates with antique-inspired curve-back chairs, their subtle upholstery urging their warm wood to centre stage. A modest gilded chandelier that borders on but misses being whimsical plays counterpoint to the formality of framed architectural prints lining the walls. No extraneous details clutter the small space.

DINING DRAMA

The marriage of contemporary and traditional elements creates frisson, giving an edge to a room and furthering its sense of drama. Mismated chairs do it here: some covered in up-to-the-minute leather, some gessoed and gilded. Ditto the table: historically derived classic column bases rendered in plaster support an inch-thick sheet of glass. Table settings combine the best of both styles; the artwork and window treatment define the room as a formal-but-friendly space. This is personal decorating at its height, created to please the owners, who delight in dining drama.

GILT TRIP

New Modern rooms often feature recycled (and redressed) items left over from another look. A glitsy gold lamé cloth with plump piping dresses up an old pedestal table, hiding its strong-but-dated seventies' origins. Four tired-out chairs become showstoppers when freshly outfitted in eye-popping but casual striped fabric. The table-and-chairs combo knocks the mickey out of the seriousness of the room, whose finely detailed plasterwork ornamentation suggests formality. Curtainless windows and bare floors also keep the focus on the furnishings.

Dining Room
PROJECTS

CHINA COLLECTIBLES

Brush up on hot-look china and glassware and display your collection on open shelves.

The sunshine colors and pretty patterns of decades-old dinnerware and decorative glass put punch in any decor ... a piece on a side table, several on a shelf. Make it a project: check out garage sales and flea markets where you're bound to find big, beautiful bargains that will make your rooms sparkle. Don't be shy: turn over pieces of pottery and find out who made them and where.

Here's what to look for:

TOP SHELF: Fabulous fifties dinnerware, designed and produced by Russel Wright and made in the U.S. under the American Modern line. Love those muted colors and fluid shapes!

SECOND SHELF: Two takes on flower-decorated chinaware. Left, a group of brightly colored Maling and Sons china, made in England in the mid-1930s. On the right, three chintz-patterned pieces of Royal Winton china, manufactured in England by Grimwades between 1930 and 1956.

THIRD SHELF: Left, Carlton Ware's Australian-designed shapes and pastel shades, made in England by Wiltshaw & Robinson between 1930 and 1950. On the right, Hollingshead & Kirkham's exuberant dinnerware and accessories, produced in England in the 1930s and 1940s.

FOURTH SHELF: Fiesta Ware in these five forthright colors, made in the U.S. by The Homer Laughlin China Company, dates from the 1930s through the 1950s. It is being reproduced today, but the colors are different.

FIFTH SHELF: Colorful Loetz pieces, made in Czechoslovakia between 1910 and 1918, appeared in strong-colored opaque glass trimmed with black or white.

BOTTOM SHELF: Left, Majolica pottery, produced by several companies in England, Europe and the U.S., between 1880 and 1930, its inspiration taken from nature's shapes and colors. On the right, Sparkling Manhattan glassware, featuring concentric rings of glass ridges, was made in the U.S. by Anchor Hocking between 1939 and 1941.

FAUX-FINISH DOOR

You don't need real wood grain when you can fake it.

SHOPPING LIST

- *oil-base eggshell paint in plum or other color for the base coat*
- *2-inch (5-cm) paintbrush for painting base coat*
- *Pratt & Lambert's Faux Finish Lyt-All Glazing or other glaze, tinted with a cream-colored pigment*
- *coarse bristle brush*
- *matte oil-base varnish*

1. Give the wood a base coat of plum oil-base paint.

2. When dry, apply the tinted glaze with a bristle brush, dragging it over the wood to create wavy lines.

3. After it dries, finish with a coat of matte oil-base varnish. Use the same technique to give old furniture a new look.

SPOT ON

Punch up a dinner party with leopard-pattern charger plates.

SHOPPING LIST

- *glass charger plates*
- *Pebeo Porcelaine 150 paints, one bottle each in the following colors: Abysse, Calcite and Dune*
- *small pointed-tip paintbrush*

1. Clean the plates thoroughly.

2. Paint on the underside of the rim. Starting with Abysse (black) paint, apply rough oval shapes, spacing as you want the spots to appear. Leave the centres unpainted. Let dry for 30 minutes.

3. Using Calcite (tan) paint, fill in the holes in black shapes. Then use Dune (sand) paint to fill in the background. Let dry for 24 hours.

4. Bake in a 300°F (150°C) oven for 35 minutes to set the paint.

HANDLE WITH COLOR

Give humble cutlery an up-market look.

SHOPPING LIST

FOR FOUR FIVE-PIECE PLACE SETTINGS:
- *stainless-steel cutlery*
- *four blocks white polymer modeling clay*
- *four blocks yellow polymer clay*
- *three blocks each of black and red polymer clay*
- *discarded rolling pin or discarded pasta maker (do not use for food after using with polymer clay)*
- *craft knife*
- *pin with round head*
- *waxed paper*
- *small wooden roller (sometimes called a brayer), 2 inches (5 cm) wide*
- *one bottle polymer-clay varnish*
- *small paintbrush*

1. For each piece of cutlery, roll out the white modeling clay to approximately ⅛ inch (3 mm) thick, using the rolling pin or pasta maker.

2. Cut to fit around each handle and press into place, smoothing so the handle is completely covered. This will give the handle some thickness when completed.

3. Bake according to the manufacturer's instructions. Let cool.

4. Make the dotted clay: roll out the yellow clay ⅛ inch (3 mm) thick. Poke indentations into the surface using the top of the round-headed pin. Roll tiny bits of black clay into small balls and place on the indentations.

5. Cover with a piece of waxed paper and roll until flat using a small roller. Use to wrap around the middle section of the handles, placing the seam at the back. Smooth the seam closed.

6. To make the striped clay, roll out a block of the red and a block of the black clay until ⅛ inch (3 mm) thick. Trim the edges so two pieces are the same size and lay one on top of the other. Cut in half and stack on top of each other again so you have four layers. Repeat once more. Press firmly so the layers stick together. Slice through the layers into pieces ⅛ inch (3 mm) thick and use to wrap around the handles at either end of the yellow centre sections. Place the seam at the back; smooth into place. Cut a thin strip of the red clay and use to cover where the yellow and striped sections join. Press into place. Bake according to the manufacturer's instructions. When cool, apply two coats of polymer-clay varnish. The cutlery may be hand-washed in lukewarm soapy water.

PLACES PLEASE

Set a colorful table with wipe-clean place mats.

SHOPPING LIST

FOR SIX PLACE MATS:
- *1 yard (1 m) No. 10 heavyweight canvas, 60 inches (1.5 m) wide*
- *three (2 oz/60 mL) bottles white acrylic craft paint*
- *pencil*
- *ruler*
- *one (2 oz/60 mL) bottle each of red, green, blue and yellow acrylic craft paint*
- *three (2 oz/60 mL) bottles acrylic craft varnish*
- *1-inch (2.5-cm) paintbrush*
- *small pointed-tip paintbrush*
- *hot-glue gun and glue sticks*
- *1½ yards (1.4 m) cotton muslin, 1 yard (1 m) wide, for backing*
- *pinking shears*
- *white craft glue*

1. Cut six pieces of canvas each 14x19 inches (35x48 cm).

2. For each place mat, pour half a bottle of white paint into a small bowl and dilute with water until it is the consistency of cream.

3. Set the canvas pieces on several layers of newspaper. Using a 1-inch (2.5-cm) paintbrush and this paint mixture, prime the surface of the canvas by painting almost to the edges. Let dry.

4. Using a pencil and ruler, mark off a rectangle 11½x17 inches (29x43 cm) on the primed canvas. Then use a pencil to trace around the diamond pattern provided. Working with one paint color at a time, use a small pointed-tip paintbrush to create the pattern within the marked lines. After the paint has dried, it may be necessary to apply a second coat to get the color especially intense.

5. Let dry, then use a 1-inch (2.5-cm) paintbrush to apply five or six coats of varnish. Let the varnish dry thoroughly between coats.

6. Cut across the corners at the outer markings of each place mat. Turn under the raw edges to the wrong side. Press down using your fingers, then glue in place using a hot glue gun.

7. Using pinking shears, cut out six pieces of cotton muslin, slightly smaller than the finished size of the place mat. Glue in place on the underside of each place mat using a thin line of craft glue around the edges.

Kitchens
TASTEFUL COOKING

THE KITCHEN is one of the best rooms in the house in which to indulge personal expression. Since it is both a work and play space, the room offers plenty of scope to be creative in making it do exactly what you want it to do.

Efficient spatial planning, sufficient storage and adequate countertop space are required. The aesthetic implementation of these become the occupants' pleasure to organize and design.

The owners of the kitchen on page 73 chose sleek contemporary lines, neutral colors and easy-care surfaces. Minimal decoration and ornamentation interrupt the smooth flow of space. In another kitchen, this one efficiently streamlined (see right), wood cabinets create an unexpected sense of warmth, and when the wood is combined with a hooked floral rug and centrally positioned antique table (masquerading as an island), it creates a New Modern space, richer for its combinations. In both these kitchens (with warm wicker and small wooden accessories in the former, old and new mixed together in the latter), the fact that everything doesn't exactly match adds invigorating interest. Otherwise, the rooms would both seem as cold and homogenized as the milk in the refrigerator.

Dining *en famille* in the kitchen is as pleasant as in the dining room when the room is as comfortably furnished as it is on pages 70 and 71. The cloth-covered table and upholstered chairs that could just as well be used in a dining room add up to comfort. In true New Modern style, it's a room that combines many materials: granite, wood, glass, tiles and stainless steel.

Kitchen projects for the decorating do-it-yourselfer take on a New Modern edge when they combine unexpected materials. Check out the checkerboard floor painted over basic plywood on page 77. Imagine, plywood! And have a peek at the terrazzo look given to basic Aspenite underlay on the flooring in the open-concept living room/kitchen on pages 41 and 73. This treatment is often given to hardwood, tile or concrete floors, but to do it on underlay is a departure, acceptable to New Modern enthusiasts. Finding new or alternate ways of using decorating materials is very much in keeping with the new style and the perfect place to use them is the kitchen. ❖

A Cook's Kitchen

A variety of natural ingredients — some sleek and shiny, some rough and textured — create a kitchen designed for a serious amateur cook. At the heart of the setting, a commercial gas stove holds court, anchored by a stainless-steel hood and backsplash. Maple cabinets, influenced by simple Shaker design, are fitted with sedate knobs and bin pulls. Granite countertops sweep around the U-shaped food-prep area and provide an elegant surface for quickie meals.

MODERN MIX

Granite, laminate, wood, ceramic tile and glass blend in a thoroughly modern kitchen, creating a warm-yet-leading-edge room. A sense of simplicity dominates the space. The clean lines suggest an efficient place to work, yet the upholstered chairs and warm colors soften the effect. Oak flooring connects the room with the rest of the house and visually expands its size.

FUSION INFLUENCED
Warm maple cabinets and cool black granite counters fuse dramatically in a kitchen for the times. More materials inject energy: stainless steel appliances, surface-mounted and pot lights in the ceiling and, for mystery, the merest hint of the cupboard contents hiding behind spectrum-glass doors. The easy-care materials throughout make the kitchen a desirable place for cooking.

KITCHEN WITH AN OUTLOOK
No one style informs the open kitchen of a renovated house, where exposed steel beams repl confining walls, and clay pots and wicker baskets warm up laminate countertops and cabinets with neoprene knobs. Modern metal bar stools cozy up for quickie meals; an antiqued armoire hides dishe The comfort of the living area is but steps away.

Kitchen
PROJECTS

CLASSY-GLASS CABINET DOORS
Catch the light with glass etching.

1. While it is easiest to work on the glass panes if they are lying on a table, it is possible to etch them while they are hanging in place. Wash the glass and dry thoroughly.

2. Attach the stencil to the glass using masking tape.

3. Wearing rubber gloves and using a wooden stick or paintbrush as an applicator, apply a thick coat of etching compound inside the stencil cut-out. Do not let any etching compound touch the glass except within the stencil. Leave for the time recommended by the manufacturer, then wash off with lukewarm water. Remove the stencil.

4. Use window cleaner and a paper towel to remove any marks and dry thoroughly.

SHOPPING LIST

- *two hardware-store cruet bottles*
- *spray-on stencil adhesive*
- *alphabet stencil*
- *latex gloves*
- *¼-inch (0.5-cm) bristle paintbrush*
- *glass-etching compound*
- *window cleaner*
- *paper towel*

ETCHED IN GLASS

Fancy up your table with decorated oil and vinegar bottles.

1. Thoroughly wash and dry the bottles.

2. Spray stencil adhesive onto the back of the stencil. Let dry until tacky.

3. Press the stencil firmly into position on the bottle.

4. Wearing latex gloves and using a small bristle brush, apply the etching compound on the glass within the stencil openings. Leave for the time recommended by the manufacturer. Wipe off under running water.

5. Remove the stencil. Clean the bottles with window cleaner and a paper towel.

DRESS UP A FLOOR

If your money runs out before you've finished your kitchen renovation, postpone installing expensive flooring and paint the plywood underlay.

SHOPPING LIST

- *wood filler*
- *sandpaper*
- *roller and paint tray*
- *oil-base floor paints in three colors*
- *Masonite cut into large and small square templates, approximately 12 inches (30 cm) square and 3 feet (1 m) square*
- *small paintbrush to outline squares*
- *medium paintbrush to paint inside lines*
- *wide paintbrush or a roller refill to apply polyurethane*
- *oil-base polyurethane*

1. Sweep the plywood floor. Fill any large cracks with wood filler; let dry, then sand them. Sweep clean.

2. Using a roller, apply two coats of white oil-base floor paint over all, allowing the first coat to dry before applying the second.

3. Have your lumberyard cut two square stencil templates out of Masonite. Determine the centre of the room. Lay the large template, on the diagonal, at the centre and use a pencil to trace around it to mark off the area to paint in a light gold color.

4. Lay the small template at each corner of the large square and trace around the areas to be painted dark gold. Repeat over the entire floor, leaving the long spaces between the squares white.

5. Apply two coats of each color. When dry, brush or roll on three coats of polyurethane to seal floor, letting dry between coats.

STENCIL MANIA

Personalize napkins with names of favorite foods.

SHOPPING LIST

- *1 yard (1 m) cotton fabric or four cotton ready-made napkins*
- *stencil brush*
- *fabric paint*
- *alphabet stencil*

1. Wash and iron the fabric. Cut into four equal squares. Iron the edges to the wrong side in a narrow double fold and machine-stitch in place. If using ready-made napkins, wash and iron.

2. Hold the stencil in place along the edge of the napkin. Dab the stencil brush in fabric paint, taking care not to overload it with paint, then jab lightly inside the stencil letters. Do not smudge the paint when removing the stencil.

3. When the paint has dried, press with a hot iron according to the instructions on the paint.

Note: If you cannot find textile paint in the color you want, you can mix acrylic craft paint with textile medium as directed on the bottle.

WINDOW DRESSING

Punch up a kitchen window frame with a padded valance.

SHOPPING LIST
- ¼-inch-thick (0.5-cm) plywood or Masonite
- jigsaw (an electric one works best)
- fine sandpaper
- fabric
- polyester quilt batting
- masking tape
- staple gun and ¼-inch (0.5-cm) staples
- cord for trim
- hot-glue gun and glue sticks
- black cotton fabric
- white craft glue
- 1½-inch-wide (4-cm) Velcro™

37 in.

21 in.

1. Measure the external dimensions of the width your window frame. Add 1 inch (2.5 cm) to each side.

2. Decide on a shape you like or use the pattern shown. Then draw your pattern, sized to fit your window's measurements, onto a large piece of paper, such as newspaper.

3. Cut it out, then trace around the pattern onto ¼-inch (0.5-cm) plywood or Masonite. Cut out around the lines using a jigsaw. Sand any rough edges.

4. Again using the pattern, cut out a piece of fabric, allowing an extra 4 inches (10 cm) of fabric all around, and a piece of polyester quilt batting, but add only 2 inches (5 cm) all around.

5. Lay the fabric wrong-side up on a large table or the floor. Place the batting on top. Lay the plywood on top of that. Pull the batting onto the wood and use masking tape to hold it in place at random points. Clip the batting where necessary to fit around curves. Pull the fabric around the board in the same way. Use a staple gun and ¼-inch (0.5-cm) staples to attach the fabric at approximately 1-inch (2.5-cm) intervals. Clip the fabric to adjust to the curves.

6. Using a hot glue gun, attach the decorative cord around the edges. Using the pattern, cut out a piece of plain black cotton fabric. Press under the raw edges. Use craft glue to attach on the back side of the valance.

7. Staple one half of a Velcro™ strip to the window frame. Staple or glue the corresponding other half onto the valance, positioning it so the valance hangs where you want it. Mount in place.

FUNKY FLOOR MAT

A painted canvas floor cloth brightens a room.

SHOPPING LIST

- *heavyweight (#10) canvas*
- *white acrylic paint*
- *2-inch (5-cm) paintbrush*
- *pencil*
- *several colors of acrylic craft paint*
- *small artists' paintbrushes*
- *acrylic varnish*
- *scissors*
- *hot-glue gun and glue sticks*

1. Cut the canvas to the desired size, adding an extra 4 inches (10 cm) to the length and width dimension for turning under the edges 1 inch (2.5 cm) and to allow for shrinkage.

2. Lay the canvas on several thicknesses of newspaper. Thin the white paint with water until it has the consistency of heavy cream. Use it to paint one side of the canvas, leaving a ¾-inch (2-cm) border unpainted. Let dry.

3. Mark the pattern on the painted canvas with a faint pencil line. Using several colors, paint as indicated or do your own design. Let dry, then apply three or four coats of acrylic varnish, allowing it to dry between coats.

4. Fold the edges to the underside and press in place using your fingers. Cut across the corners to remove some of the fabric, which will make for a neater turn. Use hot glue to hold the edges in place.

5. Wipe with a damp cloth as required.

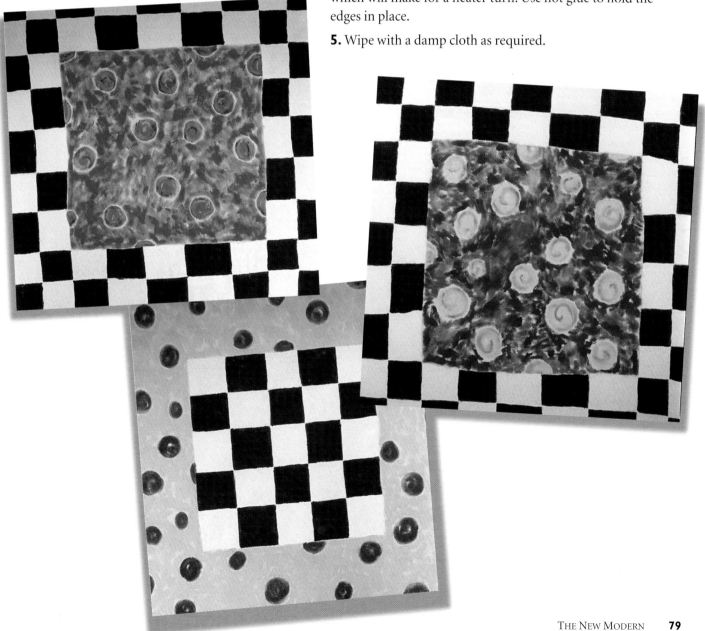

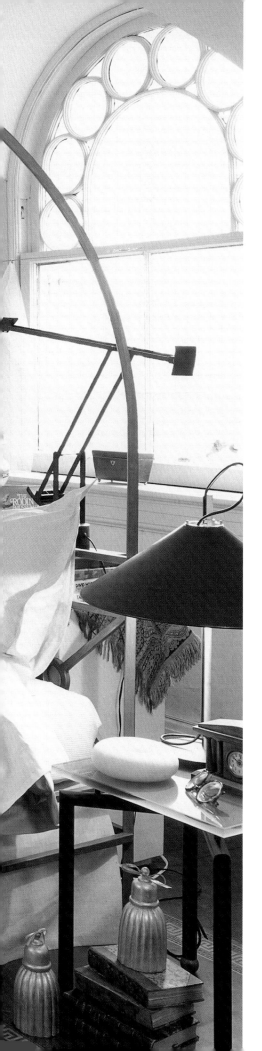

Bedrooms

SLEEPING BEAUTIES

NO ONE style of decorating defines the New Modern bedroom; the pleasure of the people who retreat there is what counts most. The rooms that follow prove this point and suggest ways of creating one's own New Modern bedroom.

Here's the place to gather together all your favorite things, as it is done in the room opposite. The eclectic mix means the eye never stops feasting on the combination of modern accessories and family-favorite heirlooms, but when relaxation is in order, a comfortable loveseat — and the bed — are ready to oblige.

If soothing calm is on the order books, three New Modern bedrooms provide examples of different ways to achieve the look. The warm color scheme and sleek lines of the headboard and the window covering of the bedroom on page 90 get it right. In a different, but equally satisying, way, so does the bedroom on page 91, where setting the bed on the diagonal uses the space creatively, and minimal accessories

THE WELL-DRESSED BEDROOM

Taking its cue from a Palladian window, a classically inspired but contemporary canopy bed dominates a bedroom filled with cherished possessions. Warm woods balance cool metals. Sheer curtains cover the broad windows. An antique urn and ironstone footbath share space with a cool modern lamp. The clever combination of old and new accessories — all in muted tones — adds cozy comfort to the subdued, restful room.

LINEN-WRAPPED LUXE

Paper-backed linen wallcovering disguises the aged walls and cracked ceiling of the sitting-area/dressing-room end of a gentleman's bedroom. Matching fabric and a matchstick blind treat a problem window with panache and visually expand the space. The folding fabric-covered screen holds personal notes — and hides an unsightly radiator from view. Metal lamps meet the warm woods of the dresser and side table. Comfort is all in this very personal space that overflows with important mementoes.

PUTTING IT ALL TOGETHER

Contemporary, country and quirky meet in a very New Modern bedroom. Tension wire stretched wall-to-wall suspends window- and closet-covering canvas. Pine chests and an oak chair (out of view) put color in an otherwise monochromatic room. Shaggy fabric covers a chair from the fifties. This mix of materials, periods and styles defines and informs the newest please-oneself decorating trend.

PILE ON THE PATTERNS
An intricate bed covering anchors a bold decorating scheme in this mix-and-match bedroom. Its mauve and orange colors reappear in patterned accessories — the gathered table skirt, rare carpet topping wall-to-wall broadloom and on the walls. Boldly striped window coverings reveal orange flounced header cuffs; leopard-print upholstery decorates bergère chairs flanking the classic fireplace. Nothing matches exactly — not even the colors — but the engaging mixture of furnishings creates a relaxed-yet-energized room.

celebrate the emptiness. The bedroom on pages 86 and 87 also invites relaxation amidst sink-into pillows surrounded by soothing taupe walls.

In the New Modern style, mixing textures is more important than mixing patterns, but when there's a combination of both, the result is dynamic and energetic, as the bedroom opposite proves. The nubby surface created by the sinuous lines of the pattern on the tablecloth complements the textures of the bed covering. The leopard-print upholstery of the bergère chairs has a soft plush nap; the window coverings are crisp and snappy. Each texture brings something to the overall success of the room. That the blue colors are not exactly the same shade adds interest— and an edge.

Textures and materials are important design elements in the bedroom on page 82, too. Antique pine furniture warms up the cream walls and wool carpet. Cotton curtains slide across tension wire to close both the window and closet wall. A fifties chair, upholstered with tufted cotton fabric, seems almost sculptural in the context of this room. ❖

BEDROOM MAGIC

Calm colors and simple furnishings provide a luxurious look in a small-scale bedroom. Classic accents such as the convex mirror and antique picture frames team up with a contemporary bed and metal lamp. A cloth-covered storage-creating shelving unit and an antique lacquer-top bamboo table bookend the bed. A treasured trunk and gathered window coverings reveal the soft side of the occupant, whose personal monogram boldly decorates one of the bed pillows.

PERSONALITY-PACKED

Myriad materials and energizing textures fuse in a happening bedroom whose occupant — a with-it teen — conscientiously endorses all things green, even the wall color. Wicker, sisal, cork and canvas back up cotton coverings on the caster-fitted bed and wood-slatted window blinds. The angled bed makes creative use of the attic space. All surfaces overflow with favorite possessions. There's no doubting the modern sensibility of the girl who lives and sleeps in this room.

WRAPPED IN WARMTH

Warm colors and sensuous textures add up
to a relaxing room. Patterns and materials
mix and mingle. A shimmering sheer Roman
shade draws attention to the wide windows.
At the front of the bed, a rustic wicker chair
cozies up to a sleek harlequin-pattern table;
a metal one sits bedside. Antique accessories
and contemporary lamps join a stack of books
on the headboard shelf (for instructions on
how to make it, see pages 94 and 95).

EDITED DOWN

Whitewashed wood and pastel colors create a comfortable bedroom in a country home, where curtainless windows reveal the trees. Stripped of all but essentials, the room loses no coziness because of the warmth of the heirloom covering on the Victorian bed, ticking-upholstered chest, and wicker tray table. It's an uncluttered room with space to breathe, eclectic but empty, simple but welcoming.

Bedroom
PROJECTS

DO-IT-YOURSELF

HIDDEN ASSETS

Create a sleek and streamlined headboard for a queen-size bed.
This is a good project if you've had some building experience.

1. Have the lumberyard cut two sheets of plywood into the following pieces: one 68x43 inches (for the back panel); two 30½x43 inches (for the front panels); and one 8¼x64 inches (for the top). Apply three coats of varnish, sanding well between coats.

2. Join the Timmy boxes in the following way, using five for each end and three for the middle stack. From inside the boxes, use four ½-inch (1-cm) wood screws to join the top of one box to the bottom of the one above. Paint the boxes, if desired.

3. Attach box stacks to wood panels. Start with the centre stack of three boxes. Screw three angle brackets to the sides of the boxes, then screw boxes to the inner edges of the two front panels. Attach the end stacks to the front panels, positioning them 2 inches (5 cm) in from the ends of the panels and 2 inches (5 cm) down from the top edge and flush with the bottom of the panel. Use ½-inch (1-cm) bolts to mount the angle brackets to the backs of the boxes and ½-inch (1-cm) wood screws to attach the angle brackets to the front wood panels.

4. Stand this up and attach the back panel by screwing through the wood into the sides of the boxes. Lay the top piece on top of the boxes and screw into the boxes to attach.

5. Drill ½-inch (1-cm) holes where steel rods are to be placed. Cut rods 11 inches (27.5 cm) long and install, holding them in place with the hex nuts and washers.

6. Install two pot lights in the top piece.

WALL-TO-WALL HEADBOARD

Build a striking headboard like the one on page 90 in an afternoon.

SHOPPING LIST

FOR THE FRAME:

• *2x2-inch pine for a frame to which to attach panels (the lumberyard dimension will likely be 1½x1½ inches).* * *Buy enough for three times the width of the room, plus four upright pieces, each 32¼ inches (80 cm), plus four cross pieces each 6 inches (15 cm) long for joining the front and back pieces of the frame at the top.*

> **Lumber from different mills is cut to different sizes, which is why it is impossible to state unconditionally that the wood will be exactly 1½x1½ inches.*

FOR THE PANELS:

• *½-inch-thick (0.5-cm) MDF (medium-density fibreboard). We used three panels, each 35 inches high (88 cm). To determine the width of the panels, measure the width of the room. Subtract 1 inch (2.5 cm) and divide by three to get the panel width. This will result in a ¼-inch (0.5-cm) space between the three panels and at the outside edges, which will create "shadow lines." For a room significantly wider than 10 feet (3 m), which ours was, you may prefer to use four panels. Adjust your measurements and lumber requirements accordingly.*

FOR THE TOP:

• *clear pine board 1x10 inches x width of the room.*
  (The lumberyard dimension may be ¾x9½ inches.)

Other supplies:
• *fine-tooth saw and level*
• *3-inch (8-cm) and 1-inch (2.5-cm) screws;
  power screwdriver*
• *1½-inch (4-cm) drill bit*
• *1½-inch (4-cm) plastic grommets*
• *Polyfilla*
• *paint and paintbrush*
• *sandpaper*

Note: The dimensions given assume that the floor is even and flat and the walls are straight and at right angles to each other. Adjust the dimensions as required to compensate for on-site conditions. Use a level to ensure the frame is square before adding the panels and the top.

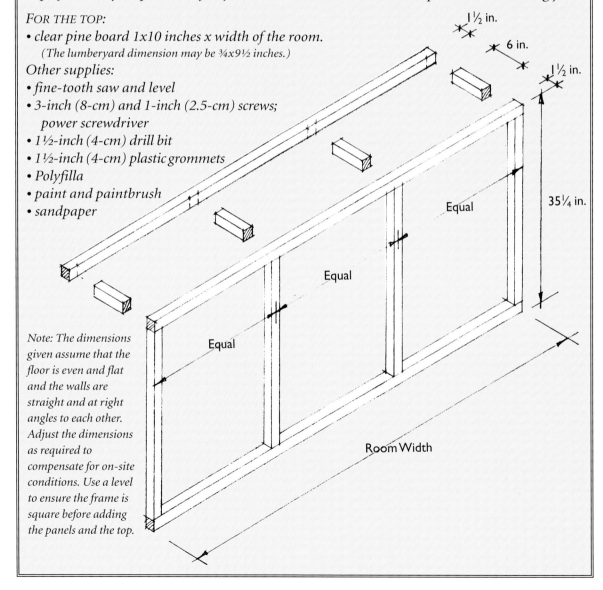

1. Remove the baseboard from the back wall. Using a fine-tooth saw, cut out and remove the side baseboards, 9 inches (22.5 cm) from the back wall.

2. Construct the front frame, using 2x2s as in the diagram. Attach the upright pieces to the long horizontal pieces with 3-inch (8-cm) screws.

3. Using a level, draw a line horizontally across the width of the back wall, 35¼ inches (88 cm) off the floor. Locate the studs in the wall; screw the top back length of 2x2s to the studs below that line, using 3-inch (8-cm) screws. Draw a line on the floor, from side wall to side wall, 9 inches from the back wall. Stand up the front frame with its front edge inside the lines. Screw the bottom of the frame to the floor every 12 inches (30 cm). Use a level to check that the frame is vertical, then screw the two end upright pieces to the side walls.

4. Insert the 6-inch-long (15-cm) cross pieces to connect the front frame to the back piece of 2x2s. Use 3-inch (8-cm) screws through the front of the frame into the ends of the cross pieces. Screw the end cross pieces into the side walls and screw each of them at an angle into the back 2x2 rail.

5. Using 1-inch (2.5-cm) screws, attach the panels to the uprights and top and bottom horizontals, positioning each panel ¼ inch (0.5 cm) below the top edge of the top framing horizontal, ¼ inch (0.5 cm) in from each end wall and ¼ inch (0.5 cm) apart. Countersink the screw heads, fill with Polyfilla and sand ready for painting.

6. If you plan to set lamps on the headboard shelf and there is an electrical outlet on that wall, proceed with Step 6. Otherwise, proceed to Step 7.

Drill holes for the electrical cords in the top board. Temporarily lay the board on top of the frame; insert the grommets into the holes, then the cords; lift up the top board and plug the cords into the electrical outlets. Replace the top.

7. Screw the top into place using 1-inch (2.5-cm) screws. Countersink the screw heads; fill with Polyfilla, sand, then paint.

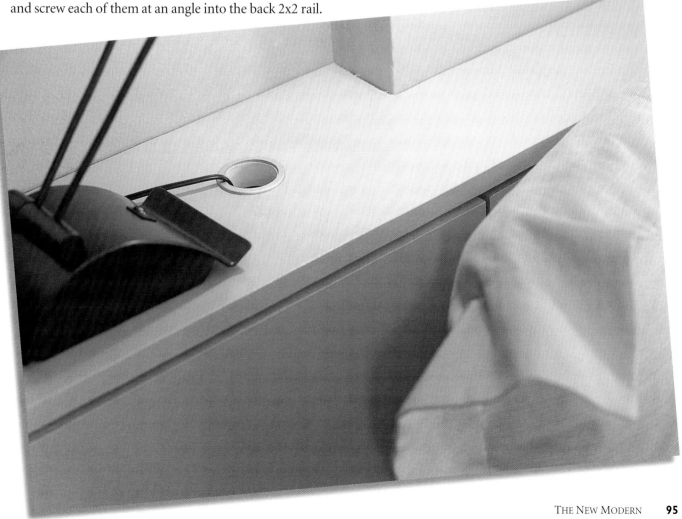

GEORGIAN CHARMER; NOT FOR SALE!

Paint a Georgian-style building on a cast-off dresser.

SHOPPING LIST

- *dresser, with at least four drawers, taller than it is wide*
- *Polyfilla*
- *medium and fine sandpaper*
- *latex primer paint*
- *several sizes of paintbrushes*
- *pencil*
- *brick-red, black and white high-gloss latex paint*
- *white plastic drawer handles*

1. If new handles do not fit the holes of existing handles, fill the holes with Polyfilla and let dry. Sand the dresser whether or not it is new, unpainted or a cast-off. Start with medium-grade sandpaper, then finish with a light rubbing with fine-grade paper. Wipe down, then paint with a coat of latex primer paint.

2. Using the picture as a guide or a picture of a favorite building, draw an outline of the details with a pencil. The drawers each represent one "storey" of the building; the handles are positioned to correspond with a white horizontal band around the "building."

3. Paint with the red-brick color first. Let dry, then use white paint to draw windows and other details. Let dry, then paint black areas.

4. Attach the drawer handles.

STRIPE IT RICH!

*Painted stripes in subtle tones
give walls a soft textured look.*

SHOPPING LIST

- *two shades of eggshell latex
  paint*
- *paint tray and roller*
- *pencil*
- *chalked plumb line*
- *painters' tape*
- *one paint roller, 2 to 3 inches
  wide (5 to 8 cm)*

1. Select two shades of paint adjacent to each other on a color-chip card.

2. Using a roller, paint the room in the lighter color. When dry, use a pencil to make a mark every 4 inches (10 cm) at the top of the wall, just below the ceiling, to indicate where your stripes will be painted. (If you want narrower or wider stripes, make these marks closer together or farther apart.)

3. Get someone to help you with the next step. Hold the string of the plumb line at one of the markings at the top of the wall so the plumb bob's point is slightly above the baseboard. Press the lower end of the string against the wall and snap the line. A line of chalk will appear on the wall. Repeat until all the lines are marked. Press painters' tape along the lines, creating 4-inch (10-cm) stripes. Use a small roller to apply second color of paint within alternating strips.

4. Carefully remove the tape as soon as the paint is dry.

WINDOW WAKE-UP!

A padded valance adds charm to a bedroom window.

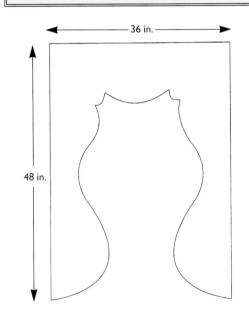

SHOPPING LIST
- *¼-inch (0.5-cm) plywood or Masonite*
- *jigsaw (an electric one works best)*
- *fine sandpaper*
- *fabric*
- *polyester quilt batting*
- *masking tape*
- *staple gun and ¼-inch (0.5-cm) staples*
- *cord for trim*
- *hot-glue gun and glue sticks*
- *black cotton fabric*
- *craft glue*
- *1½-inch-wide (4-cm) Velcro™*

36 in.

48 in.

1. Measure the external dimensions of the width of your window frame. Add 1 inch (2.5 cm) to each side.

2. Decide on a shape you like or use the pattern shown. Then draw your pattern, sized to fit your window's measurements, onto a large piece of paper, such as newspaper.

3. Cut it out, then trace around the pattern onto ¼-inch (0.5-cm) plywood or Masonite. Cut out around the lines using a jigsaw. Sand any rough edges.

4. Again using the pattern, cut out a piece of fabric, allowing an extra 4 inches (10 cm) of fabric all around, and a piece of polyester quilt batting, but add only 2 inches (5 cm) all around.

5. Lay the fabric wrong-side up on a large table or the floor. Place the batting on top. Lay the plywood on top of that. Pull the batting onto the wood and use masking tape to hold it in place at random points. Clip the batting where necessary to fit around curves. Pull the fabric around the board in the same way. Use a staple gun and ¼-inch (0.5-cm) staples to attach the fabric at approximately 1-inch (2.5 cm) intervals. Clip the fabric to adjust to the curves.

6. Using a hot glue gun, attach the decorative cord around the edges. Using the pattern, cut out a piece of plain black cotton fabric. Press under the raw edges. Use craft glue to attach on the back side of the valance.

7. Staple one half of a Velcro™ strip to the window frame. Staple or glue the corresponding half onto the valance, positioning it so the valance hangs where you want it. Mount in place.

CHEERY CHECKERBOARD

So easy to make, the kids can help create this young-at-heart cushion with its knobby-knitted trim.

1. Knit four red squares and four black squares following these instructions. Cast on 30 stitches. Knit for 7 inches (18 cm) in garter stitch (knit every row), then cast off.

2. Using wool, sew four squares together to form the pattern as pictured. Repeat for the back. Sew in the loose ends. Block each piece into a 14-inch (35-cm) square by laying them wrong-side up on an ironing board. Cover with a damp cloth, then press lightly using a low-temperature iron.

3. To make the centre rings, wind the wool around the small plastic rings until covered, then secure the end. Sew to the centre of the cushion on both the front and back, or sew on purchased buttons. Using the wool, sew three side seams together on the wrong side. Turn right-side out.

4. Stuff with the cushion form. Sew closed the remaining edge. Using a Knobby Knitter, make 56 inches (1.4 m) of trim. Use the wool to attach the trim to the cushion's edge.

SHOPPING LIST
- *Bernat Pot-O-Gold knitting worsted: two (50-g) balls red (#7225); two (50-g) balls black (#7790)*
- *pair 4.5 mm (old Canadian size 7, U.S. 7) knitting needles, or the size needed for tension of 16 stitches and 30 rows measuring 4 inches (10 cm)*
- *Knobby Knitter, available at craft stores*
- *two small rings or buttons*
- *darning needle*
- *14-inch (35-cm) cushion form*

MAKE A FLAP

Get a great texture by knitting in the linen-stitch pattern.

1. Cast on 84 stitches and work in the following pattern for the front: Row 1 (right side) slip one stitch, knit one, * bring yarn forward, slip one purlwise, yarn back, knit one *. Repeat from * to * to end. Row 2. Repeat these two rows for pattern until work measures 14 inches (35 cm). Cast off in plain knit stitch.

2. To make the back and the envelope-style flap, cast on 84 stitches and work as for the front, but continue until the piece measures 20 inches (50 cm). Cast off. Sew in the loose ends.

3. Block the pieces to fit the form by laying them wrong-side up on an ironing board. Cover with a damp cloth, then press lightly using a medium-hot iron.

4. Sew the three side seams together on the wrong side, matching lower and side edges. Turn right-side out. Sew buttons along the flap edge. Stuff with the cushion form. Tack down the flap with thread or yarn or sew on Velcro™ strips.

SHOPPING LIST
- *Kertzer's Super 10 Cotton: two (100-g) skeins ecru*
- *pair 5.5 mm (old Canadian size 5, U.S. 9) knitting needles, or the size needed for tension of 24 stitches and 32 rows measuring 4 inches (10 cm)*
- *darning needle*
- *four 1-inch (2.5-cm) buttons*
- *14-inch (35-cm) cushion form*

Bathrooms
REFRESHING SPACES

BATHROOMS ARE the perfect places to prove that a little luxury goes a long way, for most are modest in size and scale and, as a result, do not make grand statements. But this is not to suggest they should be overlooked as decorating candidates.

Bathrooms invite creative touches in wall and floor treatments, color schemes, lighting and accessorizing. Some of the most successful bathrooms found in the New Modern mode are the least "decorated." Inspect the modest bathroom opposite, for instance; its success is in its simplicity and combination of new and old elements, at least one of which had a surprising earlier life! A new pedestal sink takes its design cue from the old claw-foot tub; wainscotting and wallpaper suggest a country-inspired mood. But mixing styles in New Modern fashion, the sedate gilded mirrors have their design roots in the classical period rather than the country, and the window treatment — a lace tablecloth inherited from a grandmother — adds softness and provides privacy in a simple way.

The bathroom on page 106 also shows simple styling. Warm oak meets cool marble; classic dentil moldings style-match the owners' silver accessories. Minimal decorating is where it's at in this New Modern bath.

With comfort defining the new turn-of-the-century style, sybaritic touches assume importance. The bathroom on page 107 may be minimalist in its approach, but its materials are

SMALL-ROOM SPLURGE

A wealth of luxury fills a little space in a color-splashed powder room whose Victorian-inspired fixtures and tiles partner with classical wall sconces and a gilded mirror. Dark oak floors underpin marble-top cabinets. Sparkling brass-plate in the hardware and faucets adds another color and material to the mix.

PARED-DOWN PLUNGE

Modern materials create a traditional look in a spacious bathroom that is low on embellishments but high in style. Maple built-ins softened by a wash-and-pickle finish co-ordinate with European-style neutral-colored tiles banded in a sculpted border. A mosaic-framed mirror hangs adjacent to natural maple shutters. Chrome faucets sparkle against the prevailing wood tones. Tossed into the mix, cherished photographs and family silver decorate the top of the vanity.

RENO REFIT

The simplicity of the parts in a small bathroom contributes to its attractiveness and efficiency. Chrome pegs hold a parade of towels; a refurbished claw-foot tub gets a shower attachment refit. Tucked into the tiny window alcove, a storage cupboard and laundry chute to the basement epitomize the importance of smartly used space in New Modern interiors.

MAGIC MIX-UPS

A mix of materials and a merry mood max out a tiny bathroom that's limited by a sloping ceiling. Whimsical touches put the owner's personality at the forefront: a metal tree holds towels, a faux shirt buttons over the skylight and an industrial coiled lamp above the unadorned mirror balances a curvy candelabrum at the end of the tub.

rich and its amenities are many: the spacious frosted-glass shower stall, extra-long jet-spray tub, mirrored walls and marble-top vanity. The desire for comfort dictates the appointments in the bathroom on pages 102 and 103, whose mixed materials add up to an en-suite retreat. Visually pleasing and efficiently laid out, the bathroom easily allows two people to get ready for work or play without bumping elbows. Marble, maple and mosaics create the look. Silver accessories personalize the room.

Mixing styles and simply having fun make for a successful bath, as the challenging room below proves. Tucked under the eaves, the windowless room benefits from the installation of a skylight. But how to ensure privacy? A tailored "shirt" attached to the frame is the answer. Metal fasteners join the two panels together in the centre; when they're undone, a whimsical "collar" results. A streamlined industrial lamp

WARMED-UP MODERN
In a bathroom that shows many influences, family silver and a silvery gilt-framed mirror soften the hard edges of contemporary touches, such as chrome faucets and skinny mini-blinds. A separate shower and bathtub and warm oak cabinets boost the comfort level; dentil crown moldings add class. The overall sense is a modern minimal prettiness.

FROSTED FANTASY
Mirrors, marble, maple cabinets and frosted glass make for a sleek serene bathroom where every detail compounds the comfort level. The mix of materials and clean lines come together to enhance a small space and give it a sense of being larger than it is. Little accessory touches create warmth and personalize the space.

above the contemporary mirror balances the complex tracery of the metal towel tree. Would these elements have come together a decade ago, when a different decorating style prevailed? Not likely.

Tiny bathrooms can come off as well as large ones when they're well planned and decorated with flair. The New Modern bath on page 104 proves the point in its creative use of the small space it's given: simple panelled doors that front a cabinet created in a niche are the only ornamentation. The cabinet provides storage, and a laundry chute to the basement. No space is wasted, every inch works for its existence. ❖

Bathroom
PROJECTS

SPRUCE UP A WINDOW

Use Masonite and wallpaper to breathe life into a ho-hum window.

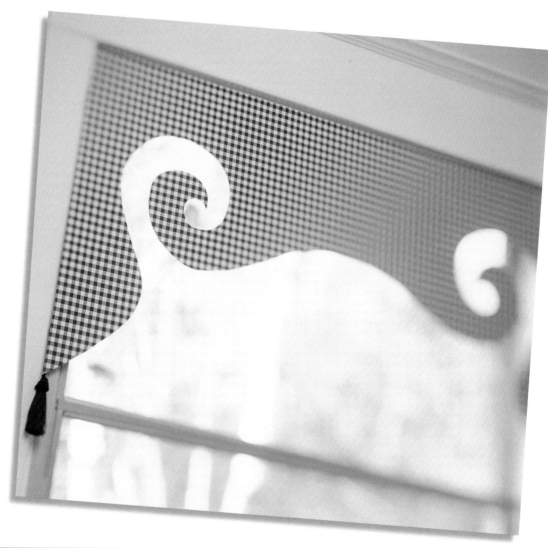

SHOPPING LIST

- ¼-inch (0.5-cm) Masonite, cut to fit the window
- wallcovering
- fret saw
- spray adhesive
- white craft glue
- sharp scissors
- tassels or other trim
- Velcro™

1. Measure the window opening.

2. Draw a design for the valance on Masonite to fit either inside or outside the window frame.

3. Use a fret saw to cut out the shape. Cut the wallcovering 1 inch (2.5 cm) larger than the Masonite shape. Use spray adhesive on the board, then press the wallpaper firmly in place.

4. Turn under the edges to the wrong side, cutting into the edges so they lie flat.

5. Glue in place using craft glue. Glue on the tassels or trim. Glue one strip of the Velcro™ to the window frame and the other strip to the Masonite. When dry, mount the valance in place.

Show-Off Shower Curtain

Stitch up a jaunty collared curtain for the shower.

1. From the striped fabric, cut one piece the width of the fabric and 73½ inches (1.9 m) long. Cut a second piece 29 inches (74 cm) wide and 73½ inches (1.9 m) long. Place the right sides together and sew together lengthwise with a ½-inch (1-cm) seam. Finish off the raw edges with a machine zigzag stitch. Turn the long side edges under ¼ inch (0.5 cm) twice and press; machine-stitch in place. Turn up the bottom hem ¼ inch (0.5 cm); press, then turn up 1 inch (2.5 cm) and press again. Stitch in place.

2. Make the piqué collar: from the white fabric, cut a piece the width of the fabric and 15½ inches (40 cm) long. Cut a second piece 28½ inches (72 cm) wide and 15½ inches (40 cm) long. With the right sides together, sew a seam to create a 72-inch (1.8-m) panel. Press the seam open. Fold the panel in half, lengthwise, right sides together. Sew the short ends together. Turn right-side out and press. Pin the open edge of the collar to the wrong side of the top raw edge of the striped fabric. Sew together with a ¼-inch (0.5-cm) seam. Flip the collar over to the right side and press. Topstitch along the folded top edge and again 1 inch (2.5 cm) below.

3. Mark places to machine-stitch 12 buttonholes for the curtain rings. The outer ones should be approximately ½ inch (1 cm) in from the side edge; the others should be spaced approximately 6½ inches (16.5 cm) apart. Sew ¾-inch (2-cm) buttonholes; cut through the fabric inside the buttonhole stitching. Tie to the shower rod with white ribbons or make small bows and attach to the shower curtain rings. The finished curtain measures 72x72 inches (1.8x1.8 m). Hang with a plastic shower-curtain liner.

COLOR-PUNCHED TOWEL BARS

A sense of fun freshens up a dated bathroom.

SHOPPING LIST
- *cordless or electric drill*
- *1-inch plywood*
- *1-inch (2.5-cm) dowel*
- *latex semigloss paint*
- *two metal bed connectors
  for each towel bar*
- *anchor plugs*

1. Use a jigsaw to cut semicircular-shaped rod holders from 1-inch-thick wood.

2. Drill holes the diameter of the towel-bar dowel in each bracket.

3. Prime and paint pieces with latex semigloss paint.

4. On each bracket back, chisel out enough wood to recess a metal bed-connector bracket. Screw in place. Insert anchor plugs in the wall. Attach screws and slide the brackets in place.

NOTHING TO SNEEZE AT!

Pop a touch of glamour in a bath or bedroom with a silvery tissue box.

1. Sand the box thoroughly until smooth. Dust off all lint.

2. Work on only one side at a time. Apply size to one surface. Set aside for approximately 30 minutes. When it feels tacky but not wet, carefully place a sheet of silver leaf onto the surface. Press in place with a soft, dry brush. Don't worry if the leaf cracks; you can stick another small piece over the hole and press down gently. Cover the surface entirely. Set aside until dry, then brush off excess leaf.

3. Repeat these steps on one side at a time. Apply the leaf to the top last.

> ## SHOPPING LIST
> - *wooden tissue box cover, available at craft stores*
> - *fine sandpaper*
> - *size (available at art stores)*
> - *1-inch (2.5-cm) paintbrush*
> - *faux silver leaf (available at art stores)*
> - *soft dry brush*

CREATIVE HOME WORK

*H*OME OFFICES appear in many forms, from a corner of the kitchen to ergonomically designed rooms that rival those inhabited by mega-conglomerate executives. But because these offices are in the workers' own homes, they can have a degree of personality that's not aways possible in a corporate environment.

For many home-office workers, possibilities are defined and limited by the amount of money available for furnishings. Obviously, technical needs must be met first (computer, printer, fax machine, etc.), followed by a good seating plan that mates appropriate desk space with the best-fitting chair the budget can manage. Then, it's up to you to create the office you want. And here's a tip: decorating the New Modern way is the best, for you can mix and match new and old, expensive and el-cheapo, eclectic or minimal.

The office on pages 112 and 115 follows these guidelines, relying heavily on furniture found in secondhand shops, a

HARD WORKING

In a home office, the worker can mix and match a blend of old and new in self-expression, for there's only one person to please. In this one, shown here and on the following page, a contemporary chair in the hottest color joins industrial shelving, the desk chair, library steps and a rolling file holder as the primary "new" pieces. A discarded school table and chairs, metal typewriter table, school lockers and a wooden table for the computer become useful-yet-funky furnishings when treated to a coat of fresh paint. Everything has its function, yet some personalizing touches creep in to make the place feel like home.

few key new pieces (such as the desk chair, soft chair and storage systems) and accessories with special meaning to the occupant. It looks streamlined, because of its size and the pared-down nature of the furnishings, but it also looks comfortable, because of the character of these accessories and personal touches.

While size is an important factor in determining how much can be accommodated in the office, big isn't necessarily better, though it opens the door for options the small office can't entertain. Locating the work space in the middle of a large room (see page 116), rather than against a wall (or in a closet, like the creative office on page 117) allows the worker vistas while sitting at the desk, and permits soft furniture for meetings.

Building a home office gradually, as money becomes available, is a route that many take. For do-it-yourselfers, the possibility to cut loose and make things is endless, and numerous projects in this chapter should inspire and instruct anyone handy with a hammer.

Whether your home office is big or small, eclectic or streamlined, one thing is certain: after you've put the pieces together, as the workers/owners of these home offices have done, it's unlikely you'll ever long for a mahogany matched set of desk, shelves, credenza and meeting table. You're in the perfect place to make a home office you want: you're going to spend eight hours a day in it, so be sure you love it. ❖

OFFICE OVERTIME

Using space creatively, a work station set up in
the middle of a room provides an opportunity
to stretch the eye in search of inspiration.
A distant fireplace and contemporary artwork
provide a feast. Upholstered chairs in the
far area make reading reports a more
comfortable experience. A structural column
becomes the basis for a shelving unit. The
simple lines of the desk encourage neatness.

CLOSET WORK

A customizing treatment turns a closet into
a wood-panelled work station, ergonomically
adjacent to a traditional desk. With the door
removed and new stained panels lining the
ceiling and walls, the former closet has an
appearance that matches the elegance of the
desk. Shelves above the computer store books
and office supplies; a light recessed into the
closet ceiling illuminates the enclosed area.

Home Office
PROJECTS

FILING CABINET WITH FINESSE

Pressed wallcovering transforms a derelict cabinet into a stunning beauty.

SHOPPING LIST
- *metal filing cabinet*
- *medium sandpaper*
- *Anaglypta wallcovering*
- *Lincrusta border wallcovering if its width will cover a drawer front completely. If not, use Anaglypta for the drawers as well as the top and sides.*
- *contact cement*
- *latex paint primer*
- *pewter colored latex paint*
- *1-inch (2.5-cm) paintbrush*
- *furniture paste wax*

1. Sand the cabinet. Cut out pieces of Anaglypta wallcovering for the top and sides, allowing enough to wrap ½ inch (1 cm) around the edges. If the Lincrusta border paper is as wide as the drawers are deep, use that to cover the fronts of the drawers. If not, use Anaglypta wallcovering, centring the pattern on the drawers.

2. Following the directions on the contact cement, attach the coverings to the top, sides and drawer fronts. Trim off any excess wallcovering.

3. When the glue has dried, paint the cabinet with a coat of primer. Let dry, then paint with two coats of pewter-colored paint, allowing to dry between coats.

4. When thoroughly dry, rub on furniture wax and buff to a soft shine.

PAPER TRAILER

Put plain wooden boxes to work in a home office.
This one holds packing supplies.

SHOPPING LIST
- *wood box*
- *fine sandpaper*
- *lightweight fancy paper, such as handmade Japanese paper*
- *white craft glue*
- *electric drill and ¼-inch (0.5-cm) drill bit (optional)*
- *¾-inch (2-cm) or 1-inch (2.5-cm) casters and screws*

1. Lightly sand the box. Cut the paper to fit the top, bottom and sides of the box, allowing ½ inch (1 cm) extra to wrap around.

2. Spread glue thinly and evenly on the front and back of the box. Press on the paper, wrapping the edges over the top edge and under to the bottom and around to the adjacent sides. Spread glue on the two end pieces. Cut the paper to fit exactly at the side corners, but leave enough to turn over at the top edge of the box and under the bottom. Attach paper to the bottom in the same way, having cut the paper to fit exactly with no overhang for wrapping around. Attach paper to the top of the box, turning under the rim edges.

3. If you plan to use the box to store packing supplies and you want to keep your cord or twine from getting tangled, drill a hole in the lid and thread the twine through it from the underside. When required, pull the twine through the hole and cut off as much as you need.

4. Screw four casters to the underside of the box, approximately 1 inch (2.5 cm) in from each corner to make it easy to move the box around.

WELL-DRESSED WINDOW
*Pared-down decorating equals
easy-to-make window coverings.*

This window treatment works where a
window is flanked by walls immediately
to either side or where the covering can
be inset into the window frame.

1. Measure the size of the window to be
covered and calculate the amount of fabric
required. You will need twice the width of the window
opening in order to provide fullness and enough extra
fabric for hems top and bottom.

2. Sew the panels together, if required, to give the correct
fullness; press the seams open. Sew double hems 1 inch
(2.5 cm) wide along the side edges. Press under ½ inch
(1 cm) at the top, then fold again to create a hem 5 inches
(12.5 cm) deep. Sew in place. If desired, a 5-inch
(12.5-cm) strip of interfacing may be ironed in place before
stitching. Press under ½ inch (1 cm) along lower edges,
then again to create a 3-inch (8-cm) hem. Sew in place.

3. Punch grommets in the top hem about 4 inches (10 cm)
below the top edge and about 8 inches (20 cm) apart.

4. Mount the hardware, thread the wire through the
grommets and hang the coverings in place.